LOVE
LOSS
LESSONS

OCTAVIA OCTAVIANO

LOVE LOSS LESSONS

Copyright © 2026 by Octavia Octaviano

Published by Octavia Octaviano

LaGrange, Georgia, USA

All rights reserved. No part of this book may be reproduced, distributed, or transmitted in any form or by any means, including photocopying, recording, or other electronic or mechanical methods, without the prior written permission of the author, except in the case of brief quotations embodied in critical reviews and certain other noncommercial uses permitted by copyright law.

Cover Design: Octavia Octaviano

First Edition, February 2026

ISBN: 978-0-692-87421-9

LCCN: 2026901721

Cataloging data prepared by the publisher.

Contents

Before Love Has a Name

I. LOVE

First Sight Isn't Always Visual

The Body Knows

Desire Without Ownership

What Woke Up

Familiarity

Magnetic

The Laugh That Did It

Attraction Isn't Always Gentle

Letting You See the Fear Habits

Learning Your Weather

The Work of Staying

Small Intimacies

Exposure

What You Know About Me Now

The Bravery of Staying

Awkward

What You Reflect

Projection

Where My Wounds Showed Up

Unhealed Places

When Affection Becomes Teacher

The Mirror Doesn't Lie

Childhood Wounds in Adult Love

Love Exposes

II. LOSS

The Exact Moment

Sudden Ending

Slow Betrayal

Where the Warmth Used to Be

When Silence Replaced Everything

You Stopped Asking

The Knowing

Fracture

Losing Versions of Myself

Time

Hope

Different Language

The Ghost of What Could've Been

Losing the Story

- Muscle Memory
- The Weight
- What Death Doesn't Cover
- Everything and Nothing
- The Rage That Feels Ugly
- Replaying Conversations
- Bargaining with Ghosts
- Wanting Closure
- The Exhaustion of Pretending
- Numb
- Anger at Myself
- When Crying Stops Working
- The Fantasy of Revenge
- Bargaining with Time
- The Quiet Brutality
- When Anger Runs Out

III. LESSONS

- Where I Saw My Own Fingerprints
- The Patterns I Didn't Want to See
- Where I Abandoned Myself
- How I Taught People to Treat Me
- Love vs. Endurance
- Accountability

The Difference

What I Ignored

Reckoning

Carrying Memory Without Letting It Steer

Sitting with Loneliness

Forgiveness Without Reconciliation

Choosing Peace

What I Keep

The Work of Integration

Learning to Sit

The Ache That Stays

Integration

Love with Boundaries

Love as Verb

The Courage to Begin Again

Love That Includes the Self

Not Naive, Not Closed

What I Know Now

The Questions I'll Ask

Quietly Hopeful

Reimagined

The Beginning

After the Lesson Has Landed

Before Love Has a Name

Some hungers arrive

before we have the words for what we're reaching toward—

just the body leaning into light,

the throat opening without permission,

the heart doing what it does

when it recognizes something

it hasn't met yet.

I.

LOVE

First Sight Isn't Always Visual

I recognized you
not by your face
but by the way you held your silence—
like someone who'd also learned
that some truths don't translate into small talk,
that some wounds make you fluent
in languages no one wants to speak.

The Body Knows

Before my mind could list the reasons,
my nervous system said *yes*—
pulse quickening at your proximity,
skin remembering touches
that hadn't happened yet,
the oldest part of my brain
lighting up at recognition:
here is someone
who smells like home
and danger
in equal measure.

Desire Without Ownership

I want to know
the architecture of your thinking,
the weather patterns of your moods,
what makes you laugh when you're alone—

but I don't need to hold the deed
to every room inside you.

What Woke Up

Something in me
that had been sleeping for years—
not dead, just dormant—
opened its eyes when you spoke.

Not love yet.
Not even attraction in the usual sense.

Just recognition.

The way a language you forgot you knew
suddenly makes sense again
when you hear it spoken
by someone who grew up
in the same kind of silence.

Familiarity

I swear I've known you before—
not in a past life,
nothing that mystical—

but in the way your anger moves,
the specific quality of your loneliness,
the jokes you make to deflect
when something gets too close to the bone.

I recognize you
because I've been you.

Magnetic

Physics doesn't explain
why certain people
rearrange the air around them,
why proximity feels like weather,
why some voices
make you want to lean in
even when the words are ordinary.

The Laugh That Did It

It wasn't your smile.
It was your laugh—
the one you tried to muffle,
the one that escaped anyway,
unpolished and real,
the sound of someone
who hadn't forgotten
how to find the absurd
in the wreckage.

Attraction Isn't Always Gentle

Sometimes desire arrives
like vertigo,
like standing at the edge
of something you could fall into
and not come back from—

and part of you knows better,
knows the drop is steep,
knows you're probably going to get hurt,

but you lean forward anyway.

Letting You See the Fear Habits

I tried to hide them at first—
the way I check my phone compulsively,
the way I go quiet when I feel cornered,
the way I apologize for taking up space,
the way I test you without meaning to,
pushing just to see if you'll stay.

Eventually I stopped performing.

Learning Your Weather

You wake up heavy some mornings,
not sad exactly, just dense—
like gravity works differently
on certain days.

I'm learning not to fix it.
Not to take it personally.
Not to fill the silence
with false cheer.

Just to sit beside you
while the weather moves through.

The Work of Staying

Love is not the feeling.
Love is the decision you remake
on the days when the feeling
has gone quiet,
when frustration sits between you
like a third person at the table,
when you're both tired
and the easy thing
would be to walk away.

Love is choosing
to stay in the room,
to keep talking,
to not let resentment
calcify into distance.

This isn't romance.
It's labor.

Small Intimacies

The way you hand me tea
before I ask for it.

The way I know
which silence means you're thinking
and which means you're hurting.

The way we've built a language
out of glances and half-sentences,
the way we don't need to finish
every thought out loud.

Exposure

To let you love me
I had to let you see me—

not the curated version,
not the one I show at parties,
but the one who cries in the car,
who sometimes hates herself,
who doesn't always know
what she needs,
who is trying
and failing
and trying again.

The risk wasn't that you'd leave.

What You Know About Me Now

You know which memories
make me go quiet.

You know the specific way
I disappear inside myself
when I feel unsafe.

You know my tells:
the forced cheerfulness,
the deflective humor,
the way I clean when I'm anxious.

You know me
past the version I perform,
and somehow
you're still here.

The Bravery of Staying

Some days loving you is easy—
the way you move through a room
makes sense to my nervous system,
your presence a gift.

Other days loving you requires
every ounce of maturity I have:
to not make your mood about me,
to let you be human and flawed,
to choose you again
even when the feeling has gone quiet.

Awkward

Nobody tells you
how awkward intimacy can be—

the fumbling,
the miscommunications,
the times you're out of sync,
the moments when you want closeness
and they need space,
or vice versa,
and you both just sit there
trying to navigate needs
that don't quite align.

What You Reflect

When I'm with you
I notice things about myself
I'd been avoiding—

how I apologize too much,
how I dim my joy
to make others comfortable,
how I've been performing confidence
instead of building it.

You don't point these things out.
You don't have to.

Projection

I thought I loved you
but I loved the version of you
I'd built in my head—

the one who would save me
from my own loneliness,
who would fill the gaps
I hadn't learned to fill myself.

You were never going to be that person.

And the moment I stopped asking you
to be my salvation,
I could finally see you:
flawed, human, real.

Where My Wounds Showed Up

I didn't know I had abandonment issues
until I watched myself
panic at your silence,
manufacture problems
to test if you'd stay,
push you away
just to see if you'd come back.

You didn't cause this.

Unhealed Places

I brought my unhealed places
to our love
and asked you to hold them
without telling you
what they were.

I expected you to know
which words would trigger me,
which actions would feel like betrayal,
which silences would resurrect old ghosts.

When Affection Becomes Teacher

Loving you taught me
where I needed to grow—

not because you demanded it,
but because your presence
showed me the gaps:

how I struggle with receiving,
how I equate love with sacrifice,
how I've confused
being needed
with being valued.

The Mirror Doesn't Lie

You reflect back
the version of me
I'm actually being,
not the one I think I'm being.

And sometimes that's uncomfortable—
seeing my defensiveness,
my patterns,
my ways of shutting down
when I feel exposed.

Childhood Wounds in Adult Love

The reason I need reassurance
has nothing to do with you.

The reason I shut down
when conflict arises
has nothing to do with you.

The reason I expect abandonment
has nothing to do with you.

You just walked into a house
where all the furniture
was already arranged
by people who left
a long time ago.

II.

LOSS

Love Exposes

Before you,
I could pretend
I had it all figured out—

that I was healed,
whole,
unbothered by the past.

But love doesn't let you hide.

It finds every place
you're still protecting yourself,
every wall you've built,
every wound you've covered
with scar tissue and distance.

The Exact Moment

I can tell you
the exact moment I knew—

not when you said the words,
not when you left,
but before that,

when I looked at you
and realized
you'd already gone,
that I'd been talking
to the memory of you
for weeks.

Sudden Ending

No warning.
No buildup.

One day we were us
and the next
we were past tense,
and my brain couldn't catch up,
kept reaching for you
in all the old places—

your name on my tongue,
your teacup on the counter,
your opinion in my head—

and finding only air.

Slow Betrayal

It wasn't one big thing.

It was the accumulation
of small abandonments:

promises softened into maybes,
maybes dissolved into silence,
silence hardened into distance,

until one day I looked up
and you were a stranger
wearing a familiar face.

Where the Warmth Used to Be

I kept returning to the spot
where we used to sit,
expecting the light to feel the same,
expecting something
to remain—

but the warmth was gone.

Just cold stone.

When Silence Replaced Everything

We used to talk for hours.

Then the hours became minutes.
The minutes became small talk.
The small talk became silence.

You Stopped Asking

You stopped asking
how my day was,
stopped noticing when I was quiet,
stopped reaching for my hand
in the car on the way home.

And I didn't say anything
because I thought maybe
I was being needy,
maybe I was imagining it,
maybe if I just waited
you'd come back.

The Knowing

My body knew first—

the way my stomach dropped
when your name appeared on my phone,
the way I started bracing
for disappointment,
the way I stopped sharing
the good things
because I couldn't trust
you'd care.

I didn't want to believe it.

But the body doesn't lie.

Fracture

One moment
we were whole.

The next,
a crack appeared—

thin at first,
almost invisible,
the kind you could ignore
if you wanted to.

But cracks don't stay small.

Losing Versions of Myself

I don't just grieve you.

I grieve the version of me
who believed in us,
who planned a future
with your name in it,
who thought love
could be enough.

She's gone now.

And I miss her—
her hope,
her certainty,
her refusal to see
what was already ending.

Time

I'm grieving the time—

the years I gave,
the hours I spent
trying to fix what was broken,
the mornings I woke up hopeful,
the nights I went to bed pretending
everything was fine.

Hope

The hardest thing I lost
wasn't you.

It was the hope
that I could love someone
and not lose myself in the process,
that I could be seen
and not abandoned,
that I could trust
and not be betrayed.

Different Language

I loved you in English.
You loved me in silence.

And we both pretended
that was translation enough.

The Ghost of What Could've Been

I'm not grieving who you were.

I'm grieving who I thought you'd become,
the future I mapped out in my mind,
the life we were supposed to build,
the promises that never materialized.

I'm mourning a person
who never existed.

Losing the Story

We had a story.

I knew it by heart—
how we met,
what we survived,
where we were going.

And now I don't know
what to do with it.

Do I rewrite the ending?
Do I burn the whole thing?
Do I keep it
as a cautionary tale?

Muscle Memory

My body keeps forgetting
you're not here—

reaching for you in sleep,
turning to tell you something
when the kettle whistles,
expecting your voice
to answer.

Grief, I'm learning,
isn't just emotional.

It's physical.

It lives in the nerve endings,
in the habit of reaching,
in the muscle memory
of a life that no longer exists.

The Weight

Some days grief is a stone
I carry in my chest.

Other days it's a fog
I move through.

And some days
it's just weight—
the heaviness of waking up
and remembering
all over again
that you're gone.

What Death Doesn't Cover

We don't talk enough
about the grief that comes
from losing someone
who's still alive—

the way they haunt you
from a distance,
the way you can't mourn them properly
because they're still out there
living a life
that doesn't include you.

It's a strange kind of loss.

Everything and Nothing

I lost everything.

And also:
I lost nothing of real value.

Both are true.

And I don't know
which truth to hold.

The Rage That Feels Ugly

I'm angry.

Not sad.
Not wistful.
Not gracefully accepting.

Angry.

The kind that makes my hands shake,
that makes me want to scream in the car,
that makes me rehearse arguments
I'll never have the chance to deliver.

This isn't the kind of anger
you polish into a poem.

Replaying Conversations

I replay every conversation,
searching for the moment
I could've said something different,
the moment I could've caught the glass
before it shattered,
the moment where if I'd been
smarter, kinder, less needy,
maybe you would've stayed.

I know this is useless.
I know it's a loop
that leads nowhere.

But I can't stop.

Bargaining with Ghosts

If I text you,
maybe you'll remember what we had.

If I change,
maybe you'll come back.

If I wait long enough,
maybe you'll realize
you made a mistake.

I'm bargaining with someone
who isn't listening,
offering terms to a ghost.

Wanting Closure

I want you to explain it—
to sit down and tell me
exactly when you stopped loving me,
exactly what I did wrong,
exactly what changed.

I want a neat ending,
a satisfying answer,
a reason that makes sense.

The Exhaustion of Pretending

I'm tired of pretending I'm fine.

Tired of smiling when people ask how I'm doing.
Tired of saying "I'm good" when I'm not.
Tired of performing recovery
for people who need me
to be okay.

Numb

Some days I don't feel anything—

not sad,
not angry,
not even empty.

Just… numb.

Like my body ran out of feelings
and decided to shut down
until further notice.

And it scares me.

Anger at Myself

I'm not just angry at you.

I'm angry at myself—

for staying too long,
for ignoring the signs,
for believing your promises,
for making excuses,
for sacrificing my needs
to keep the peace,
for giving you chance after chance
when you'd already shown me
who you were.

That's the anger
that's hardest to sit with.

When Crying Stops Working

I used to cry and feel better.

Now I just cry
and feel tired.

The tears don't release anything anymore.
They don't bring relief.

They just… happen.

The Fantasy of Revenge

Sometimes I imagine
running into you
when I'm thriving—

when I'm happy,
when I'm glowing,
when I've become
the version of myself
you said I'd never be.

And I imagine you regretting it.

I know this is petty.

Bargaining with Time

Just one more day of this.
Then I'll feel better.

Just one more week.
Then I'll stop checking your social media.

Just one more month.
Then I'll be over it.

I keep bargaining with time,
asking it to move faster,
asking it to dull the edges.

The Quiet Brutality

What no one tells you
is how boring grief can be—

the same thoughts on repeat,
the same ache in the same place,
the same longing with nowhere to go.

It's not dramatic.
It's not cinematic.

It's just the quiet brutality
of waking up every day
and having to live
without the person you built your life around.

III.

LESSONS

When Anger Runs Out

Eventually,
the anger runs out.

Not because you've healed,
not because you've forgiven,
but because you're just...
tired.

Tired of carrying it.
Tired of feeding it.

So you let it go.

Not because you're ready.

Because holding on
is exhausting.

Where I Saw My Own Fingerprints

I spent so long
blaming you for the ending
that I didn't notice
my own fingerprints
on the fracture.

I stayed when I should've left.
I silenced myself to keep the peace.
I made myself small
to make you comfortable.

You didn't force me to do that.

I chose it.

The Patterns I Didn't Want to See

This isn't the first time
I've loved someone
who couldn't meet me.

It's not the first time
I've given more than I got.

It's not the first time
I've mistaken endurance for love.

At some point,
I have to stop calling this coincidence.

Where I Abandoned Myself

I abandoned myself
every time I said "I'm fine"
when I wasn't.

Every time I swallowed my anger
to avoid conflict.

Every time I made excuses
for behavior that hurt me.

Every time I prioritized your comfort
over my own truth.

You didn't abandon me.

I did.

How I Taught People to Treat Me

I taught you
that my boundaries were negotiable.

I taught you
that my needs could wait.

I taught you
that I'd tolerate anything
as long as you stayed.

Love vs. Endurance

I thought love meant staying.

I thought love meant sacrifice.

Love meant
enduring whatever came
and calling it commitment.

Accountability

I can't change what you did.

But I can own
what I allowed,
what I ignored,
what I tolerated
in the name of keeping you.

The Difference

The difference between love and need
is this:

Love lets the other person be who they are.

Need requires them to be
who you wish they were.

I needed you.

What I Ignored

The signs were there.

The distance.
The excuses.
The way you stopped showing up.

I saw them.

But I explained them away,
made allowances,
gave you the benefit of the doubt
long past the point
where doubt was reasonable.

Reckoning

This is the hard part—

not grieving you,
but facing myself,
seeing clearly
where I participated
in my own heartbreak.

Not because I deserved it.

Carrying Memory Without Letting It Steer

I carry the memory of you
like I carry old scars—

present,
but not in charge.

I don't need to forget you
to move forward.

Sitting with Loneliness

I used to fill the silence
with anyone
who would sit in it with me.

Now I'm learning
to be alone—

not lonely,
just alone.

To sit with my own company
and not run from it,
to let the quiet be quiet.

Forgiveness Without Reconciliation

I forgive you.

Some days.

Other days I rehearse your name
like a weapon,
practice speeches
you'll never hear,
imagine confrontations
that will never happen.

Forgiveness isn't linear.

It's just something I keep choosing
when I have the strength for it.

Choosing Peace

Peace doesn't mean
pretending it didn't hurt.

Peace means
I can think of you
without my hands going cold,
without my body bracing
for a door that isn't there anymore.

Most days.

What I Keep

I don't have to erase you
to heal from you.

I can keep the good parts—
the laughter,
the lessons,
the moments that mattered—

and still leave behind
what no longer serves me.

The Work of Integration

Integration is unglamorous.

It's not a moment of clarity.
It's not a sudden breakthrough.

It's just the slow work
of taking what hurt you
and making it part of your story
without letting it become
the whole story.

Some days I fail at this.

Learning to Sit

I'm learning to sit with discomfort—

to let feelings move through me
without rushing to fix them,
to hold grief and gratitude
in the same breath.

Some days I can't do it.

The Ache That Stays

There's an ache that never fully goes away—

not sharp anymore,
not debilitating,
just a quiet sadness
that lives in the back
of my awareness.

I used to think healing meant
making it disappear.

Now I know
it just means learning
to carry it.

I think.

Integration

I am not the same person
who loved you.

I am not the same person
who lost you.

I am someone new—
built from the same materials,
but arranged differently.

And some days I don't recognize her.

Love with Boundaries

Next time,
I will love with boundaries—

not walls,
but clear lines
that say *this far and no further*.

At least that's what I tell myself.

I don't know yet
if I'm strong enough
to hold them.

Love as Verb

Love isn't what you feel.

It's what you do—

the showing up,
the honoring of needs,
the choosing again
on the days when the feeling
has gone quiet.

I understand this now.

Understanding it
and living it
are different things.

The Courage to Begin Again

It would be easier
to stay closed.

To build walls so high
no one could climb them.

To decide that love
isn't worth the risk.

But I don't want that life.

So I'll stay open—
carefully,
with boundaries in place—

and some days
that feels like courage.

Other days
it just feels like fear
with better marketing.

Love That Includes the Self

Next time,
I will not pour from an empty cup.

I will not sacrifice my peace
to keep someone comfortable.

I will not shrink myself
to make room for someone else.

Next time,
love will include me too.

I've said this before.

I'm saying it again
because maybe this time
I'll believe it.

Not Naive, Not Closed

I'm not naive anymore—
I know love can hurt,
I know people leave,
I know promises break.

But I'm not closed off either.

I'm just careful.

I'm just trying to be careful.

I'm not sure I know
what careful looks like yet.

What I Know Now

The first time someone raises their voice at me now,
my body leaves before my mouth does.

The Questions I'll Ask

I won't ask *do I love them*.

I'll ask:
Do they see me?
Do they honor my boundaries?
Do they show up when it's hard?
Do they choose me
the way I choose them?

These feel like the right questions.

I hope I remember them
when chemistry tries to convince me
they don't matter.

Quietly Hopeful

I still believe in love.

Not the version I used to believe in—
the one that saves you,
the one that completes you—

but a quieter version:

love as partnership,
love as choice,
love as two whole people
deciding to build something together.

At least I'm trying to believe in that.

Some days it feels possible.

Reimagined

I'm reimagining love—

not as fairy tale or fantasy,
not as need or salvation,
but as something steadier:

a choice made daily,
a respect given freely,
a partnership built slowly.

This version of love
won't look like the movies.

But it might actually last.

Or it might not.

And maybe that's okay too.

The Beginning

I used to think
the goal was to find someone
who would never hurt me.

Now I know
the goal is to become someone
who can love fully
without losing herself.

I'm not there yet.

But I'm learning
what it feels like
to walk toward it.

After the Lesson Has Landed

The heart is not
a fragile thing.

It breaks.

And it mends itself
in the breaking,
grows something new
in the fracture.

I am not who I was
before the breaking.

I am someone quieter,
less interested in intensity
and more interested in truth.

And if I love again,
I will love differently.

I think.

I still flinch when the door closes too hard.

But I don't mistake that
for the body leaning into light anymore.

www.ingramcontent.com/pod-product-compliance
Lightning Source LLC
Chambersburg PA
CBHW022019290426
44109CB00015B/1243